Original title:
The Walls That Remember

Copyright © 2025 Creative Arts Management OÜ
All rights reserved.

Author: Fiona Harrington
ISBN HARDBACK: 978-1-80587-132-3
ISBN PAPERBACK: 978-1-80587-602-1

Reflections of Lives Once Led

In a house where whispers creep,
There's a sock that took a leap.
It traveled far, or so it claims,
Chasing dreams and playing games.

A spoon once danced, oh what a sight,
Twisting tales 'neath the moonlight.
But now it's rusty, gathering dust,
While forks just laugh, 'cause they were just.

Fading Imprints in Echoing Halls

In the hallway, shadows sway,
Dusty memories come out to play.
A lonely shoe from long ago,
Still searching for its lost toe.

The echoes giggle, they love to tease,
Reminding chairs of the ancient sneeze.
Ghosts of dinners, and spilled red wine,
Laughing at the good ol' times.

The Guitar of Silence in Echoed Stories

A guitar sits, strings all frayed,
Once it strummed, but now it's swayed.
The stories it told of dances bold,
Now just echoes, tired and cold.

In its silence, a tickle remains,
Of ancient tunes and silly refrains.
A melody stuck, in a dusty nook,
Waiting for fingers to take a look.

Conversations of Silence Amongst the Tiles

Underfoot, the tiles all gossip,
Of clumsy feet and tasty droppings.
Each crack holds secrets, some quite funny,
Like the time someone slipped – oh how sunny!

The grout shakes hands in a silent cheer,
Joining in laughter, drawing near.
While mops complain, they still hold sway,
It's a party of dirt, hip-hip hooray!

Chronicles Inscribed in Dust

In a house where dust bunnies play,
Stories linger from yesterday's fray.
Couches hold secrets of pillows once full,
While light bulbs whisper, "Don't touch, you'll pull!"

A cat's crossed them with a pounce and a leap,
Creating a saga that's destined to keep.
Even the fridge hums a tune of its own,
As leftovers plot to reclaim their throne.

Layers of Time and Silence

Behind the wallpaper, tales are entwined,
Of socks that went missing, and bologna unkind.
The floors creak like crickets, they sing high and low,
As the chairs gossip secrets of folks long ago.

A light switch clicks, and the echo resounds,
Reminding us of the goofy clowns found.
Grandpa's old slippers laugh as they sway,
In the layers of silence, where memories play.

Ghosts Beneath the Plaster

Some ghosts are friendly, some would just tease,
Like the one who tickles your toes when you sneeze.
They dance on the ceiling, they giggle and glide,
Telling old stories of when they would hide.

With a sprinkle of dust, they waltz through the air,
Around potted plants that just don't seem to care.
If you listen real close, they might tell a joke,
About the time the cat tried to give a yoke!

Remnants of Voices Past

In every corner, echoes of laughter resound,
From grand feasts to games where the win was renowned.

Old photo frames chuckle, remembering the ball,
While mirrors just sigh, 'We've seen it all!'

The kitchen whispers secrets of cookies gone wrong,
As aprons recall flour fights all night long.
"Remember that time?" a distant echo insists,
As spoons clink together like a mischievous twist.

Whispers of Forgotten Voices

In the corner, a chair, quite bold,
With tales of the ghosts that it's told.
It creaks and it sighs, what a chat,
While sharing a joke with my old cat.

Echoes of laughter drift through the air,
Of a time when nobody cared a spare.
Home to the socks that always run,
Those memories are sticky like bubblegum!

Memories Encased in Silence

Here's a cupboard that's half full of dust,
Lurking memories, a musty old crust.
It holds grandma's bread that's gone awry,
And biscuits that could double as bricks, oh my!

The fridge hums low, a cooling breeze,
With leftover pizza, if you please.
But beware the milk, it's aged with grace,
It's a true wild card! Don't lose the race!

Where Time Leaves Its Mark

On the floor, there's a stain of red stew,
A map of my mishaps, it honestly grew.
Is that food from last week or a wartime art?
A modern Picasso, right from the heart!

The clock ticks with snickers and teasing chimes,
Just like my neighbor, with questionable rhymes.
Talk about drama, as time takes its play,
I'm ready for break time! Time, please delay!

Stories Embedded in Brick

These bricks have seen lovers, and seen their fights,
With whispers of passion at peculiar nights.
They've watched every dance, every fall, every win,
Like a silent partner in this quirky din.

With a flick of the dust, new tales arise,
Of laundry days dampened by sock surprise.
Each crack holds a chuckle, a clever debate,
The walls are alive, they just can't relate!

Glances of the Past Framed in Light

Photos hang, a little crooked,
Grandma's laugh, forever hooked.
Dad's old shirt, pulled tight and round,
Echoes of mischief all around.

A cat named Whiskers in a hat,
Tiptoeing softly, oh how he sat.
Uncle Joe, with cake on his nose,
Those silly moments nobody knows.

A dance party with orange juice,
In pajamas, looking most profuse.
Light stirs memories on the wall,
A grand old time, we had a ball!

Surprises wrapped in dusty frames,
Silly dances and made-up names.
Time tickles as we reminisce,
With every grin, we can't resist.

The Silhouettes of Stories Untold

Figures cast in shadows dance,
Old tales prance like a silly chance.
Mom's stories spin in moonlit beams,
Giggles rise like laughter dreams.

A brother who once claimed to fly,
With bedsheet wings, he hit the sky.
Falling down amidst loud shouts,
The laugh track played, no room for doubts.

Forever caught in wobbly poses,
Grandpa's stories and broken noses.
Silly whispers swirl like dust,
Memories tickling, oh, what a must!

The clock strikes fun in different hues,
Each echo tells of silly views.
Joy relives in every crescent,
Delight in laughter, oh how pleasant!

Ghostly Impressions on Wooden Beams

Wooden floors creak like a joke,
As shadows laugh and spirits poke.
The old chair rocks, a squeaky tune,
Tickling air beneath the moon.

Silly faces in woodgrain smiles,
Echoed laughter travels miles.
A ghostly wink from dusty frames,
As memories dance in timeless games.

In the attic, treasures hide,
Tattered toys and a forgotten ride.
A faded hat from days of yore,
Worn by laughs, tales we adore.

Chairs that spin, then sit back tight,
As if they join the giggly fight.
An old home, a host of cheer,
Ghostly fun, we hold so dear.

Flickering Ghost Lights of Yore

Bouncing beams under eaves and vines,
Flickering tales fall in funny lines.
A split second of giggles on air,
Impressionist memories everywhere!

Flicks of light, like winking eyes,
Every blink a new surprise.
An old dog sniffs where kids once played,
In corners where secrets were long laid.

Glowing moments from ages past,
A floating laugh, so free, so fast.
In every shadow, a chuckle rings,
Echoing softly like hidden flings.

With every flicker, the stories unfold,
Of silly pranks and fortunes bold.
Ghostly echoes, forever bright,
Dance in beams of playful light.

Archives of the Forgotten

In a dusty corner, they stand tall,
Where memories linger, both great and small.
A sock with a story, a shoe with a grin,
Whispering tales of where they've been.

Each crack in the plaster holds laughter and sighs,
Old postcards from places with questionable pies.
The cat's mighty leap from the shelf to the floor,
Left tales of mischief we still can't ignore.

Murmurs in the Mortar

Listen closely, the bricks might jest,
With echoes of chaos and untamed zest.
A squirrel once debated a rat in the hall,
Both claiming they'd conquer the not-so-tall wall.

The paint chips in chorus, a colorful tune,
Of misaligned pictures and rogue afternoon.
When the wind sighs softly, it's often a snore,
Reminding us gently to laugh a bit more.

The Timeless Echo Chamber

In this chamber of echoes, the fun never quits,
With stories of blunders and accidental hits.
A dance with the shadows, a slip on the rug,
The walls giggle softly, giving a shrug.

Whispers of laughter bounce off the floors,
As ancient tales waltz through dusty old doors.
The light fixtures chuckle, the curtains all sway,
Creating a circus of memories at play.

Timeworn Tales of Resilience

These aged stones chuckle, they've seen it all,
From epic fails to a cat's sudden fall.
When dinner went wrong, and dinner guests fled,
The walls just keep laughing, they never see dread.

Yet amidst all the humor, a lesson will rise,
That even old structures can wear a surprise.
For every lost shoe and every spilled wine,
The heart of the home will always align.

Footprints in the Dust of Forgotten Rooms

In corners where dust bunnies play,
Old socks have been lost, oh what a display.
A chair creaks a tune that's never on charts,
As memories dance in these rickety parts.

A cat looks around with a grave, furry face,
Dodging the ghosts of this cluttered space.
Forgotten toys whisper stories of youth,
While dust mites plot mischief, uncouth.

Each step unveils secrets laid bare,
With giggles and chuckles still lingering there.
A pop-up surprise, a moldy old shoe,
Where was it last seen? Let's hope it's not blue!

Yet here in the dust, there's laughter to find,
A treasure trove of the quirky and blind.
Memories giggle, they jump and they sway,
In rooms that remember the fun bits of play.

The Palette of Time on Dusty Walls

Paint splatters whisper of colors now faded,
Artistic endeavors that once were paraded.
The brush dipped in stories, each stroke busts out,
A gallery of giggles, and maybe some doubt.

Splatters of laughter, a rainbow of clumsiness,
Each hue has a tale, some pure absurdness.
The blue looks like sadness, or maybe just stew,
And red? That's for ketchup that splattered from you!

The canvas adjusts as we twist and we twirl,
In a tapestry vibrant, where memories unfurl.
A green blur of chaos, a pink burst of cheer,
What joy do we find each time we draw near?

So let's stroll through this gallery of time,
Each corner a chuckle, a rhyme wrapped in grime.
With every brushstroke a memory's grin,
On dusty walls where the fun does begin.

Echoing Heartbeats of Memory

In halls where echoes laugh and then play,
Each thud and each pat has something to say.
Bouncing off walls, those heartbeats so sly,
A symphony whispers, nostalgia on high.

A belly laugh bursts like confetti in spring,
While echoes of clumsiness begin to take wing.
Tripping through moments on wobbly feet,
Each mishap a story, oh what a treat!

In shadows where friendships learned how to dance,
Each heart skip a beat, a hilarious chance.
The ceiling fans giggle at stories now near,
While memories chuckle and draw us all here.

So listen intently to the ruckus around,
In echoes of laughter, life takes the crown.
With every heartbeat, a punchline in sight,
We dance through the moments that make us feel light.

Treading Lightly on Lost Years

We tiptoe through times that have slipped through the glass,
On years that have lingered, oh how they amass.
With each gentle step, we're careful not to bump,
In a jigsaw of stories, we'll never quite clump.

Stepping on memories, oh watch where you tread,
For lost years are tricky, they've stories to shed.
A wink from a mischief, a nod from a cap,
Where silliness wanders, we'll find a way back.

The footsteps of laughter are lighter than air,
Each patter a chuckle, we're happy to share.
Through twists of the past, our giggles collide,
In a dance with the moments we always abide.

So let's tread lightly through each fumbled year,
With laughter our compass, we'll navigate here.
For in every lost second, we find something great,
In the playground of time, we'll celebrate fate.

Portraits of the Past in Every Crack

In every crack, a tale is seen,
A warrior's dance in waxy sheen.
Histories whisper with cheeky glee,
Even the ghosts have planned a spree.

The cobblestones chuckle, oh what a sight,
As knights trip over, oh what a plight!
With a clatter and clang, they start to wail,
As past meets present in a bumpy trail.

Old paint drips laughter, oh what a riot,
A jester's grin in the glow of daylight.
The shadows gossip as stories unfold,
While echoes erupt in bursts of gold.

So when you walk by, give a nod,
To ancient quirks that have been quite odd.
Those cracks hold secrets, some funny, some sad,
Each step you take, don't be too mad!

The Murmurs of History Beneath Footsteps

With every step, a giggling sigh,
Echoes of jesters who once flew high.
The pavement chuckles, shakes with delight,
Tales of the clumsy who took to flight.

Murmurs of mischief rise from below,
As footsteps shuffle to and fro.
Maybe a tap dance or a soft shoe,
The ground remembers every miscue.

Old bricks squint with a wry little smirk,
Watching the tourists as they lurk.
Blunders abound, like comical fate,
As the past just laughs at our current state.

So tread lightly, walk with a grin,
For each misstep is laughter within.
The murmurs of history lead the way,
In this merry dance of what was yesterday.

Veils of Memory Amongst the Stones

Veils of laughter shroud the old stones,
Behind every crevice, a joke moans.
With mossy hats and a twisty grin,
The past appears, craving to spin.

A sassy statue winks with a gleam,
How many poses can one old stone beam?
Memories weave, in puddles they bask,
In a riddle wrapped tight, it's quite the task.

Ghostly fables dance in moonlight's glow,
As pebbles hum songs from long ago.
With a ladle of whimsy and a dash of cheer,
The veils of memory keep the laughter near.

So linger a while, let your mind roam,
For in the stones, there's humor and home.
Dance with the echoes, share a good laugh,
In this timeless tapestry of the past's half.

A Tapestry of Time in Every Corner

In corners where shadows take a peek,
Lay threads of laughter, both chuckles and squeaks.
History hugs, but with playful jest,
Inviting you in for a comical fest.

Patching together the tales that excite,
From bungling heroes in the dead of night.
Every twist and turn holds something bizarre,
A tapestry woven with threads of guffaw.

Witty whispers dance in the air,
Every creak and crack leads to a dare.
With winks from the past, they prod and tease,
Encouraging smiles with the greatest of ease.

So delve into corners, let laughter ignite,
For time's tapestry is a riotous sight.
With threads that connect the giggles and fun,
In every corner, the past's still not done.

The Hushed Testaments of Inhabitance

In corners where dust bunnies spin,
Old jokes are the start of a grin.
The picture frames gather dust,
They whisper secrets, that's a must.

The mice hold court, on the old chair,
Telling tales of the couch affair.
They laugh as they nibble on crumbs,
While house plants nod to forgotten chums.

The door creaks back with a sigh,
As memories of laughter fly high.
"Who left the window wide open?" they say,
"Let's air out the past and play!"

Through the crevices, echoes loom,
Ghosts of guests who left too soon.
In this merry menagerie, they convene,
Sharing punchlines where they once had been.

Requiem for Forgotten Lives

Beneath the stairs, old boots collect dust,
Once they marched with vigor, oh the trust!
Now they sit, with laces all tangled,
Chasing shadows, they've really wrangled.

A hat hangs low, in a corner it droops,
Once held high, it led all the troops.
Clothing drapes like ghosts in a jest,
"Wear me again for a special quest!"

Once there were dances, laughter did soar,
Now it's just echoes and squeaks of the floor.
Every room holds a story to tell,
In this gallery where memories dwell.

With each creak of wood, a punchline unfolds,
Regaling the days that were brave and bold.
A requiem that dances with glee,
For forgotten lives who laugh with me.

Echoes of the Past

In the attic, a banjo's off-key,
Plays the song of a cat and a bee.
They dance on the beams, defying the dust,
While the old-fashioned clock ticks with rust.

Cans of soup from years gone by,
Whisper tales of Grandma's pie.
"Did you hear the one about the dog?"
Oh those echoes, a sweet fog.

Photos fade like a hilarious dream,
Capturing moments, a whimsical stream.
Tickled by time, they all take a bow,
As laughter encircles the dilapidated house.

In the corners, the shadows sway,
Telling the jokes of youth and play.
Each echo a giggle, a side-splitting blast,
Funny how time makes the moments last.

Shadows in the Stone

Where the garden gnomes once held court,
Now just shadows and laughter retort.
They nod at the weeds with a wink,
"Let's reminisce over a drink!"

The fountain's running, but it's gone dry,
Fish tales whisper and time seems to fly.
A trowel left by an absent hand,
Dreams of a garden that never did stand.

Each pebble a story, each crack a jest,
In the fabric of time, they once were blessed.
"Hey! Who's there?" a mouse squeaks in fright,
"Is it just me, or did the moon feel bright?"

With giggles that ripple across aged stone,
These shadows recall what we've outgrown.
A funny little dance, with the past on show,
In this curious garden where memories grow.

Fleeting Whispers of Old Embraces

In the cracks, laughter hides,
Echoes of hugs, a joyful ride.
Worn edges, a secret spree,
Tickling tales of you and me.

Dusty corners, a dance or two,
Fleeting moments, nothing new.
Funny faces, we can't forget,
Giggling shadows, our duet.

Footprints swirling, lost and found,
Every step, a giggly sound.
Silly stories on faded paint,
Whispers of love, they never fade.

In these halls, a clownish jest,
Memories drift, they never rest.
With chuckles trapped in chipped facade,
We laugh again, our hearts applaud.

Memory's Touch in Each Stoic Step

Each step echoes, a playful churn,
With every quip, the corners turn.
Laughter lingered, on well-worn floors,
A dance with ghosts, through open doors.

The banter hangs, like fragrant air,
Mismatched socks and silly hair.
Time tickles, each creak and groan,
Old jokes sealed in bricks and stone.

In shadows bright, more giggles bloom,
A treasure trove in every room.
Slapstick slips on memory's stage,
A funny fable on every page.

With every sigh, a chuckle lends,
In stately walls, the humor bends.
What once was solemn, now flows with glee,
As whispers dance, we laugh with glee.

Traces of Lives on Weathered Surfaces

Smudged fingerprints, a doodle spree,
Graffiti hearts with a touch of glee.
On peeling paint, stories unfold,
Ticklish tales of love retold.

Every scuff tells a joke or prank,
Abracadabra from some silly shank.
Worn-out textures, a canvas bright,
Where laughter's hues shine through the night.

A splotch of ketchup, a pet's wild chase,
Each mark a giggle, a warm embrace.
In every corner, a chuckle pops,
As layers whisper, the fun never stops.

Slapdash stories on weathered walls,
Silly dances in the echoing halls.
Nostalgia tickles, we can't ignore,
These playful traces we all adore.

The Breath of Yesterday's Dreams

In dreams we wove, a tapestry bright,
Laughter echoed into the night.
Frolicking visions dance without fear,
As whimsy whispers, "We're still here!"

With each twilight, a chuckle peeks,
Surreal scenes, as the moonlight speaks.
Yesterday's giggles swirl in delight,
A carousel ride, oh what a sight!

Silly stews of thoughts collide,
In dreamland's play, we laugh and slide.
Funny faces in slumber's embrace,
We race through time, a comical chase.

With every yawn, a smile breaks free,
In the shadows, we sip on glee.
Recalling dreams, a merry tune,
As life unfolds beneath the moon.

Fragments of Yesterdays

Lost socks tell tales of a wild chase,
Forgotten lunches in a dusty case.
Rats in the attic have a squeaky scheme,
Stashing old memories in a cheese-filled dream.

The fridge hums softly a forgotten song,
While pickles dance nightly, don't get me wrong.
Dust bunnies gossip in corners, they tease,
Remarking on life with a dash of cheese.

Postcards from places I never have seen,
Telling tall stories like they've been to the queen.
The lamp by the window flickers with glee,
Watching me stumble in my own comedy.

In this crazy house, every nook is a muse,
They laugh at my stumbles, my quirky life blues.
Ghosts of odd moments are up to their tricks,
As I shuffle through yesterdays, plotting their mix.

History Woven in Shadows

In the cupboard lurks a sneaky old mug,
Stuffed with old napkins and a hot dog bug.
Each plate's a portrait of dinners gone wrong,
Where spaghetti dances and sings a loud song.

Dusty old shoes lean against the old wall,
Whisper of parties—oh, how they recall!
The carpet giggles with each step I take,
As I trip on the stories, a funny old ache.

Creaky old stairs tell their jokes with a squeak,
Sharing their secrets to anyone weak.
A cat in the corner rolls eyes with disdain,
Mocking my memories, they're doing it again!

Under the table, an ancient old sock,
Part of a duo that's lost to the clock.
What stories you hide beneath layers of time,
I'd laugh till I cry if they weren't so sublime!

Silhouettes Against the Silence

A chair in the corner wears dust like a hat,
Pondering moments—it's old and it's fat.
The empty mugs wink with a frothy embrace,
Recall every giggle, every funny face.

Old hats on the wall nod and they scheme,
Conspiring with shadows—what a wild dream!
With every sunset, they burst into cheer,
As night turns their stories to whispers sincere.

Bouncing on couches, old springs sound a tune,
Each plop and each plunk, a nostalgic cartoon.
The clock ticks in rhythm, it's keeping the score,
As laughter echoes from the cracks in the floor.

Oh, how the curtains sway with a grin,
Dancing with memories that gather within.
Each shadow a player, each flicker an act,
In the theater of laughter where silence is cracked.

Reflections in Stony Stillness

In the garden, a statue with a serious pose,
Hiding a smile 'neath a thorny rose.
The bench tells of secrets shared under the stars,
While squirrels plot mischief, nutty little memoirs.

A pebble rolls over, it chuckles with pride,
Claiming the stories it's carefully spied.
Frogs croak in chorus, they sing the past's tune,
As ladybugs twirl like they're dancing on June.

The old pathway groans underfoot as I stroll,
Every crack holds a giggle, each bump a new role.
The trees stand still, yet their branches can sway,
Whispering tales of the bright and the gray.

Oh, the laughs in the stillness, the joy in the pause,
Moments like jewels, without any cause.
Here in this space, where the silly doth throng,
Reside all the echoes of the light-hearted song.

Resonating Tales among the Beams

In the attic, there's a squirrel,
Hiding treasures, what a whirl!
Old shoes and hats, with tales to share,
Laughing echoes fill the air.

Each creak and crack tells a jest,
Whispers of time's peculiar quest.
The cat's meow joins the song,
A symphony where all belong.

Dust dances in a playful spree,
As memories giggle like a bee.
The floorboards sway and click their feet,
Who knew the past could be so sweet?

A crooked picture frame smiles bright,
Captures the laughter, pure delight.
With every glance, a grin appears,
These wandering tales, worth all your cheers.

Breathe Life into Abandoned Stories

In the corner, an old boot waits,
Tales of mud and garden dates.
A rickety chair spins a lore,
Of kids who played, and stuck to the floor.

Cobwebs shimmer, a lacey veil,
Hiding secrets in every detail.
A forgotten doll winks and sighs,
As shadows dance and memories rise.

A rusty toy train puffs in glee,
"Choo-choo!" it giggles, running free.
Tales emerge with every tick,
In this land where laughter's thick.

So gather 'round, let stories unfold,
In the remnants of life far and old.
We breathe with joy and quirky charm,
In every nook, a friendly warm.

Colors of Memory Coated in Dust

Paintbrushes rest with splashed dreams,
Whispers of color burst at the seams.
Old cans of paint, some gone dry,
A rainbow of thoughts that never die.

In a box, a crayon holds tight,
Sketches of days burned bright with light.
Each hue recalls an evening fair,
Laughter and joy bouncing in the air.

Frames hold scenes of silly poses,
Hats askew, like blooming roses.
Portraits that giggle with every glance,
Time wraps them in a merry dance.

So dip and swirl in this whimsical hue,
Every shade tells a tale anew.
In dust and colors, we find delight,
Resurrecting joy from morning to night.

Suspended Pasts in Every Heartbeat

In the garden, weeds sing a tune,
Of a shy pumpkin that forgot to bloom.
Squirrels tell tales of acorn heists,
While the wind chuckles, laughing twice.

Each stone in the path whispers a name,
Echoes of laughter, never the same.
A yellow butterfly flits with flair,
Winking knowingly from mid-air.

Old swing sets groan with playful glee,
As friends once swung so wild and free.
In the stillness, hearts softly thump,
Life and laughter, an eternal pump.

In each heartbeat, memories swish,
Glad to relive every silly wish.
With joy we recall the simple past,
Suspended moments that forever last.

Beneath the Surface of Silence

In whispers of old, the bricks seem to grin,
Recalling the times when we danced in our skin.
Laughter echoed loud, fond memories in tow,
As the paint peeled away, the secrets would flow.

A cat walks by, with a knowing sly look,
Did it hide a romance or a new favorite book?
In corners, a ghost with a sock on its head,
Is it fashion or function? We'll never be fed.

Combatting the dust, we waged war on the years,
Conversations with shadows, yet nobody hears.
A chorus of memories, sing soft in the night,
The walls are the witnesses, ever polite.

So here's to the echoes, the laughter we find,
In the creaks of the floor, our past intertwined.
Embrace every patch, every mark, every line,
For in these odd stories, we're all just divine.

The Keepers of Lost Dreams

Underneath the pavers, where wishes once soared,
Sat a wildly ambitious, yet underpaid bard.
He penned all his hopes with a crayon and cheer,
Now his verses are stuck, but they rarely appear.

In hallways forgotten, two socks had a chat,
One claimed it was royal, the other a brat.
Lost dreams in the cracks, having tea with the dust,
They giggle and snicker, but never combust.

Once a shoe spoke loudly, but fell from its grace,
Now it's a monument—oh, what a disgrace!
Dust bunnies are tossing a quiche in the air,
"Watch us now, folks, as we flip without care!"

So let's toast the dreams that still twirl in the dark,
To the giggles of fabric, the life of a lark.
For in corners and nooks, laughter sprinkles like dew,
Amongst lost hopes and socks, there's always a clue.

Memories Encased in Concrete

In the slab beneath us, where pizza once dwelt,
A party of memories, all still finely felt.
Old congo lines thrive in the dance of the ants,
As solo cups whisper, "You should take a chance!"

Stacked up against ages, a heap of old chairs,
Holding court with the echoes of jovial flares.
Concrete confessions, tales buried deep inside,
Where the neighbors' complaints never dared to abide.

A fountain of giggles, the bricks crack a smile,
They remember the joys from the last great while.
The mischief of children hid under the stairs,
As they plotted their schemes with sticky candy snares.

So raise up a glass to this fortress of cheer,
For walls made of whispers, we hold so near.
Each chip is a laugh, each scrape tells a tale,
Here's to misfortune, may our laughter prevail!

Remembrances in the Quiet

In corners of calm, where the echoes now sleep,
Resides a long cat, with a sinister creep.
It watches the dust bunnies, party all night,
With the spoons from the kitchen, tucked in close, oh so tight.

A coat hangs neglected, on a once-thrilled hook,
It witnessed wild dances, oh, the fun that it took!
In shadows it chuckles, along with the moon,
"A toast to our antics—maybe someday soon!"

Old riddles and rhymes get trapped in the beams,
As the floors creak aloud, sometimes cooler than dreams.
Oh, the places we've been to, the lives we have led,
In silence, the stories still dance in our head!

So let laughter unravel all knotted despair,
Memories encased in the stillness we share.
For even in quiet, the fun never dies,
With a wink to the walls, we'll soar to the skies!

Foundations of Forgotten Farewells

In the shadows of the past they dwell,
Whispers in the cracks, a curious spell.
They chuckle at the plans that once took flight,
But now they're just a punchline lost to night.

Pigeons strut like they own the scene,
Critiquing echoes, if you know what I mean.
They coo with glee at the history of blunders,
As humans trudge past, lost in their plunders.

Dust bunnies dance, a whimsical crew,
Holding court where rotting memories stew.
Watch out for the ghosts, they love to play trick,
With stories that end with a humorous kick.

Feel free to stop, share a laugh or two,
These foundations have tales they'll share with you.
Laughter rings here, even after the falls,
In places where time just giggles and sprawls.

Haunting Melodies in Nature's Cradle

The trees hum a tune, slightly off-key,
While squirrels provide backup, full of glee.
A serenade from the roots to the skies,
With notes that tickle the ears and the thighs.

Frogs leap in rhythm, a comical show,
As crickets strum strings with a flair we don't know.
They sing of old trees that wear funny hats,
And mischief by owls, oh, those classy cats!

Nature giggles as it serenely sways,
While squirrels drop acorns, ruining our days.
A waltz through the wild, so absurd yet grand,
Dancing on roots, unplanned by the hand.

Listen closely, and you might hear a quip,
As the wind whispers secrets on each playful trip.
In nature's embrace, laughter flows free,
A symphony played on this whimsical spree.

The Sighs of History in Overlooked Places

In corners where dust collects like a friend,
Old hats and old socks have stories to lend.
They sigh with a chuckle for each little tale,
From socks that went missing to hats set to sail.

Echoes of laughter float through the halls,
As crumbled posters recall past balls.
They take small bets on who's coming around,
While chairs silently groan under memories found.

Did you hear the floorboards with their giggling creaks?
They gossip like children about the past weeks.
They're happy to share with a thud and a clap,
Stories of chaos lurk under each gap.

So tiptoe in gently, give them a cheer,
Let the sighs of the ages be music to hear.
A treasure trove of chuckles in every crack,
In corners forgotten, where laughter won't lack.

Portraits of Silence Amidst the Stone

Statues stand still, but they really can chat,
With pigeons as critics, they'd rate this and that.
Their features are set in a comical pose,
With stories so wild, who really knows?

The gargoyle grins, spitting tales from above,
Of villagers hoping for laughter and love.
While the pedestal's base holds the weight of a grin,
Who knew such a block had so much within?

In silent stillness, the humor runs deep,
As old stones reminisce while locals just peep.
A chuckle caught here where silence may reign,
In portraits that whisper of joy wrapped in pain.

So tip your hat to the figures in sight,
For hidden jesters can lighten the night.
In every cold face, there's warmth to uncover,
As laughter echoes beneath the stone cover.

Portraits Beneath the Plaster

In hidden frames where laughter glows,
A mustached cat wears a velvet nose.
Faded whispers of a dance so grand,
The great aunt twirled, but lost her stand.

Underneath a hat that's slightly askew,
A painter's mishap in a vibrant hue.
Each brushstroke tells of a party undone,
With clumsy moves, and a pie that won.

Lurking shadows of a jester's grin,
Why is the chicken still stuck in spin?
Oh, the stories lodged in every nook,
Where curtains creak like a gossiping book.

In a corner lies a mystery bland,
Did Grandpa eat popcorn or throw it by hand?
The past might chuckle, it's full of cheer,
With a wink of fate and a splash of beer.

Chronicles of the Unheard

Beneath the surface, silence sings,
Of flying cats and carrot flings.
A curious squirrel, bold as brass,
Dreams of racing a, you know, fat ass.

A mural sprawls with quirky scenes,
Ninjas battling in greasy cuisine.
But somewhere lost in the brush and bloom,
A taco truck forgot to zoom!

Old chairs sit with tales to share,
Does anyone remember that time in the air?
The fridge played host to a feisty toast,
That danced off the shelf, oh what a boast!

Every crack is a giggle, every scuff a laugh,
From tall tales spun from a slice of half.
Yet here we stand, with ears quite keen,
Hearing echoes of what's never seen.

Secrets Written in the Dust

In dusty corners, secrets play,
A raccoon's tale from a bright buffet.
The crumbs of laughter linger light,
As a sneeze erupts in the middle of night.

Caked-on stories of mismatched socks,
Grandma's knitting turning into blocks.
A family recipe gone astray,
When "dough" became a doughnut ballet.

Chasing shadows that giggle and peek,
The old broom laughs while the dust sneaks.
Atop high shelves, forgotten and shy,
A pickle jar's gaze meets a pancake's cry.

Each layer thick with memory's tidbit,
Dripping with humor, we ponder and sit.
For beneath the grime is laughter so bold,
In a world where the stories never grow old.

Resilient Echoes of Yesteryears

In a room where echoes twirl and dance,
The sock puppet reigns in a silly romance.
Once a king now a floppy clown,
Even the ceiling fan wears a crown.

Beneath the laughter of a well-worn shoe,
Lay tales of a pizza that almost flew.
The chandelier shakes as it starts to hum,
Did someone order a side of rum?

Framed photographs share a secret grin,
Of Uncle Joe and his sparkling gin.
The floorboards squeak with a whispering cheer,
As the past peeks in, oh what a peer!

With every story told, we chuckle and clap,
The mischief of time in a cozy lap.
For in the mess of memories hanging clear,
Lies the joy of yesteryears, we hold dear.

Lost Lullabies in Ruined Halls

In the shadows where echoes play,
Forgotten songs drift far away.
A baby's tune, now an old refrain,
That chases dust like a runaway train.

Windows whisper of dreams gone stale,
As curtains wave a ghostly veil.
What once was sweet is now quite strange,
A concert hall for the odd and deranged.

Tiny footpaths from past to now,
Small feet scamper, oh, where are they now?
Their tiny giggles, a haunting trace,
In this laughter-filled, abandoned space.

So crib the memories, wrap them tight,
In soft shadows playing hide and seek at night.
The walls giggle, they won't let go,
Of lullabies sung long, long ago.

The Ghosts of Living Rooms Past

In a plush chair sits a spectral bloke,
Adjusting his specs with a little poke.
He cracks a joke, though no one's around,
In the living room where silence is found.

A rug that remembers a spilled glass of wine,
Each stain a story that shimmers and shines.
The TV once blared, now goes dark,
It rolls its eyes at the faded spark.

The dust bunnies tango without a care,
They twirl and they swirl, oh, what a pair!
The cushions conspire to hold back a laugh,
While knitting together a forgotten craft.

So let's raise a toast to this ghostly affair,
With whispers of laughter still hanging in air.
For from the past, they cling and they dash,
In a living room filled with echoes that clash.

Counters and Corners of Remembrance

On the kitchen counter, crumbs reside,
Holding secrets they can't abide.
Each sprinkle tells tales of meals once bright,
Now only shining under the moonlight.

Corners carry whispers of a chocolate spree,
When a cake was baked, no one could see.
A spatula grins, oh what a delight,
It flipped so many pancakes, all out of spite!

The fridge hums a tune of things long past,
With mystery leftovers that never quite last.
Magnet poems jingle in quirky codes,
Each a reminder of forgotten roads.

So gather the memories, let laughter arise,
In crumb-strewn corners beneath curious skies.
For every spill has a glorious tale,
Of counters that giggle and never grow stale.

The Unfolding Layer of Time

In folds of fabric, stories reside,
A quilt of mishaps we can't let slide.
Each patch a laugh, a poke, a tease,
Stitched with moments that aim to please.

Ticking clocks can't hold back giggles,
As they count down silly little wiggles.
With each tick-tock, memory refresh,
Of days spent lost in a glorious mesh.

A calendar hangs with dates gone wild,
Reminding us of the antics of a child.
Each creased page holds a raucous cheer,
For moments that danced and wouldn't disappear.

So let's roll back to all those times,
With laughter ringing in radiant rhymes.
Through layers of time, we chuckle and sigh,
In a tapestry woven with joy that won't die.

The Canvas of Lost Journeys

In the attic, dust bunnies play,
Listening to stories from yesterday.
Old shoes and hats, a mismatched pair,
Whispering secrets we barely dare.

A suitcase grins with a handle gone,
Dreams of vacation to places unknown.
Mismatched postcards lie side by side,
Chasing horizons where friends confide.

The umbrella laughs at the rainy plight,
Remembering summers that felt just right.
Yet here it sways, lost in shoe racks,
Chatting with socks that never relax.

A rubber chicken takes center stage,
Telling tall tales of the fun age.
With every quack, a giggle erupts,
In this quirky space where joy finally erupts.

Unseen Narratives in the Grain

On wooden beams, whispers entrap,
Carpenter jokes like a skilled chap.
Each knot a riddle, each crack a pun,
Timber tickles from the deals done.

Tables have seen quite the feast,
With spills and thrills, from the bird to the beast.
Napkin tales told by a clumsy host,
Every stain a laugh, we love them the most.

Chairs squeak lies of lively debate,
While cushions plot how to rejuvenate.
A cat named Whiskers thinks he's too grand,
Dramatic diva of the land.

At the hearth, old spoons share a grin,
As the kettle hums a jazzy din.
Every creak in this old wood frame,
Is merely a chuckle, calling your name.

Reverberations of a Bygone Era

Old radios crackle with tunes long gone,
Dancing with memories until the dawn.
A grandfather clock ticks with style,
Chiming punchlines that stretch a mile.

Pictures hang crooked on the wall,
Feeling the gravity of the years' call.
Gramps in a sombrero, what a sight!
The tales of his youth, fake left, right!

A jukebox hums in laughter's glow,
As vinyl spins with an elegant flow.
Each scratchy note, a wink and a nod,
Catching the rhythm of a life once trod.

Rugs roll up to join the fun,
Matching wits with a mischievous pun.
Echoes ricochet round the hall,
A punchline marathon, come one, come all!

The Echo Chamber of History

In every corner, a giggle hides,
While ancient voices pull up their rides.
A bookcase shakes with a silent cheer,
As dusty tomes share secrets unclear.

Lights flicker in a comedic play,
Throwing shadows of a past ballet.
Ghostly jesters juggling time,
As laughter drips like sweetened lime.

The chandelier chuckles when the wind blows,
With each gust, a story it knows.
Candles whisper of parties so bright,
As laughter dances into the night.

Memento mori, yet full of glee,
History flips with a wink and a spree.
In this echo chamber, we find delight,
For memories tickle, oh what a sight!

Echoes Within Stone

In a house made of brick, once lived a cat,
Who often debated with a well-worn mat.
Each corner was packed with secrets galore,
But laughed at the ghosts who just couldn't score.

The wallpaper grinned, hung loose and all free,
Said 'I've seen more than one mystery!'
The floorboards creaked in an old-timey beat,
Making history sound like a tap dance feat.

From attic to basement, they laughed and they cheered,
While rats joined in, looking slightly unclear.
"If the walls could talk, what tales they would weave!
But alas, they've got no tales up their sleeve."

So here's to the stones, with their echoing laughs,
That remember the flops and applaud all the gaffs.
While laughter remains, oh so ripe and so ripe,
History's punchlines never lose their type.

Shadows of Forgotten Echoes

In the cellar so dark, where nobody peeks,
Lurks a shadow who giggles, disguising its squeaks.
It whispers to floorboards about old time slips,
And shares juicy gossip about the rats' road trips.

"Did you hear the one 'bout the vase and the spill?
That family nearly exploded, what a thrill!"
The shadows chuckle over a broken old chair,
Where stories once lived, now just dust in the air.

But beneath all the dirt, there's humor so fine,
With skeletons laughing over aged old wine.
"Oh, remember the ghost that danced in the night?
Turns out he tripped on his own floppy light!"

So here's to the echoes, that fade but won't cease,
With shadows that giggle, they start a new lease.
From long-buried jokes to the quirks of the past,
Each tale sends shivers, but we laugh till we gasp.

Memory's Silent Guardians

In a hallway so thick, where whispers reside,
Stand guardians watching with bulging great pride.
They guard all the secrets of toe-tapping shoes,
And tickle the funny bones of old-fashioned blues.

They snicker and smile, with each passage shared,
Reminding you once of the times that you dared.
The echoes of laughter, like rumbles of thunder,
"Remember that time? Oh, we tore it asunder!"

"Each mark on our ground tells a tale dressed in cheer,
Of swimmers who jumped, then fell in mid-air."
There's chatter and giggles in play every night,
As memories dance in the soft, glowing light.

So thank you, dear walls, for your patience so grand,
For the stories we make and the laughter we hand.
Silent guardians keeping our joy in the fold,
We're never too serious; we let our tales unfold.

Whispers Through the Brick

If bricks could whisper, they'd share all the lore,
Of folks who once stumbled and blushed on the floor.
With laughter they'd tell of the wiggle and sway,
The time Uncle Joe spun too fast in the fray.

Each crack holds a giggle, each crevice a joke,
About mishaps and mayhem that made the walls choke.
"Oh, that moldy old pizza, it surely was king,
'Twas perched on the shelf like a strange pizza thing!"

The chimneys would chime in with tales from afar,
Of chefs who flipped pancakes straight into the car.
And windows would nod with delightful surprise,
At the shenanigans sneaking through their white eyes.

So next time you pass where the bricks seem to lean,
Remember the laughter, the joy that resides unseen.
For in every old wall, there's a humor so thick,
Echoing chuckles… yes, whispers through the brick.

A Symphony of Echoes in Hollow Spaces

In a room full of echoes, I tiptoe around,
Each creak of the floorboards is quite a loud sound.
A ghost with a quip, he rattles my bones,
While I swear my own jokes are way better known.

The paintings are chatting, their frames in a twist,
They gossip about each other, oh what a mist!
I overheard one say, 'That shade is so bland,'
As I stifle my laughter and try to withstand.

Beneath the old chandelier, dust bunnies prance,
They dance with abandon, who knew they could dance?
While I sip on my tea, I can't help but grin,
At the antics performed by the dust balls within.

With each passing moment, the echoes grow bright,
A symphony of laughter fills up the dim light.
The walls hold the stories, the silly and sweet,
In this charming abode, where the funny times meet.

Merging Shadows On Timeless Paths

In the shadowy corners, the whispers collide,
Like old friends who met in a laughter-filled ride.
They crack up together, retelling old tales,
Of how one lost his shoe, and the other lost scales.

The hallway is bustling, with footsteps unseen,
A parade of lost socks, oh what a routine!
They trip and they tumble, all over the floor,
An ankle-biting army, in search of a door.

A mischievous light flickers, it plays peek-a-boo,
It feigns like a child, so cheeky and true.
While shadows are merging, they're plotting away,
To prank all the guests when the night turns to day.

These paths that we wander, so timeless and grand,
Are filled with the laughter from a whimsical band.
Each step leads to madness, each turn leads to fun,
In this playful embrace, we're forever young.

Footfalls of Time on Aging Floors

Every time I step out, the floor boards protest,
They creak like a geriatric in need of a rest.
Yet somehow they giggle, with each little moan,
'You think you're so spry, but you've only grown prone!'

The carpets they chuckle, plush with delight,
And the shadows join in for a midnight bite.
They swap all the stories of slippers and shoes,
While I try to tune in to their curious blues.

With every footfall, the house shakes its head,
'This place is a saga, you've no clue,' it said.
As I dance through the rooms like an uncoordinated bird,
The laughter and memories collide and are heard.

So here's to the footsteps that keep us in check,
To the wisdom of ages in every creak's deck.
With humor as fuel, this old house stays alive,
In the footfalls of time, where the quirky can thrive.

Haunting the Edges of Memory

In a corner, the cat takes a nap,
Remembers the fish that slipped through a gap.
The box of old toys sits, dustily grinning,
While shadows of laughter keep playfully spinning.

Grandpa's old hat, it wobbles and sways,
Recalling the tales of long-ago days.
With a wink and a twist, it tiptoes along,
Echoes of mischief in a comical song.

Peering through pictures, a burst of delight,
Uncle Joe's pants that once fit just right.
The squeaky old floorboards join in the fun,
With creaks and with cracks telling jokes 'til we're done.

Memories dance with a bounce and a cheer,
While ghosts in the back laugh and sip on their beer.
Though echoes may fade, the chuckles won't cease,
As time gently giggles, granting us peace.

Scripted in the Dust

A dusty old book with pages unturned,
Holds tales of lost socks and bowls that were burned.
Every word whispers secrets and sighs,
As cobwebs salute with mischievous eyes.

The clock on the shelf ticks in silly ways,
Counting the moments and slacking some days.
A sassy old chair creaks wise with a yawn,
While dreams play peek-a-boo, trying to dawn.

Pictures on walls seem to smirk and jest,
Replaying the highlights of each silly quest.
Naps on the couch, snacks in the dark,
They seem to chortle at each little spark.

Our laughter is woven, like threads in a quilt,
While dust settles slowly, with no hint of guilt.
The stories within these four messy walls,
Breathe life into echoes, wherever time calls.

A Tapestry of Ghostly Whispers

A ghost in the garden sips tea with a grin,
Recalling the times when it partied within.
Fences of whispers and gossipy trees,
Tell tales of mischief on a whimsical breeze.

Lurking in shadows, the sunflowers sway,
Plotting their hijinks for a lighthearted play.
With roots intertwined, they chuckle aloud,
As crickets and sparrows gather a crowd.

Raccoons with masks hold a late-night parade,
While owls debate if last night's light raid.
The breeze carries stories of fun and delight,
As moonlight enlivens the mischief-filled night.

In this quilt of remembrance, laughter's the thread,
Stitched close to moments that never quite fled.
So gather your tales, let them twirl and caper,
For memories dance like a whimsical paper.

Inner Sanctums of Time

In the attic, where forgotten things hide,
A tricycle waits with a grin far and wide.
Dustings of laughter spin tales from the past,
As echoes of giggles forever hold fast.

Old board games sit in a charming disarray,
With pieces that wander, lost in their play.
The checkered board chuckles at the time gone by,
As memories shuffle and giggles comply.

Each corner is filled with a curious stare,
While chairs hold their breath, quietly aware.
In the nooks and the crannies, adventures unfold,
As time weaves a tapestry, bright and bold.

So raise a toast to the fables we keep,
For laughter's the treasure that we long to reap.
In the sanctums of time, the fun never ends,
As we share all the stories, with laughter, our friends.

Patterns of Memory in the Mortar

In bricks there lies a tale so bright,
Of laughter echoing through the night.
They whisper secrets, sly and bold,
Of socks and shoes, and stories told.

Cracks and chips, a dance of cheer,
Caught on camera, don't come near!
A teenage crush, a winter's bliss,
Forgotten kisses, we reminisce.

The plaster still holds grandma's stew,
And stains from where the cat once flew.
With every dent, a sketch of glee,
A home that joins in memory's spree.

So let's toast to the giggles shared,
With walls that stood when no one cared.
They glimmer with hope and childhood dreams,
In the mortar, life bursts at the seams.

The Timeless Witness of Structure

Oh, the beams know all my silly laughs,
Like ticklish toes, and funny gaffs.
Wind that whirls like a dancing sock,
Every creak is a chuckle, tick-tock.

With paint so old it dabs and blinks,
Underneath, the ceiling winks.
They've seen us trip on clumsy feet,
Falling over as we try to greet.

Each corner holds a giggling fight,
And shadows that dance throughout the night.
If voices could bounce off of floors,
We'd hear our dreams behind closed doors.

Oh, structures tall, you've seen it all,
The highs, the lows, the big and small.
You stand quite proud, your stories spin,
With laughter echoing, how could we not grin?

Fragments of Souls in Confined Spaces

Inside the nooks where echoes play,
With memories that never sway.
A tattered book, a toy that squeaks,
In silent halls, it softly peeks.

Each space contains a hint of fun,
With every glance, a race begun.
The mischief caught in every crack,
Where chaos meets a calm, laid back.

Silly shouts from down the hall,
The oddest dance, a leap and fall.
Invisible friends, they come and go,
In fragments keeping joy aglow.

The coziness of a couch embraced,
Where all our quirks can be traced.
In confined spaces full of cheer,
We smile at fragments held so dear.

Remnants of Life in the Atrium

With sunshine spills, and dust that sways,
The atrium holds our goofy days.
We run in circles, laugh like fools,
Amidst the plants, we ditch the rules.

The fountain splashes like our giggles,
While echoing past silly wiggles.
Remnants of joy in every nook,
A love story in every look.

Old chairs recline with tales to tell,
Of popcorn nights, and sneaky smells.
The vines climb high, as if in on,
The silly secrets we've drawn upon.

So here we gather, hearts laid bare,
Making memories, light as air.
In radiant corners, we intertwine,
Amidst remnants, life is a grand design.

Hidden Truths Behind the Panels

Behind each panel, laughter dwells,
A secret chat 'tween dusty shells.
They whisper tales of socks misplaced,
And every crumb that time has graced.

Nail holes giggle, trapped in time,
With stories of the cat's last crime.
Furniture's dance leaves creaky trails,
As echoes stifle giggles and wails.

The curtains nod to grand affairs,
Where once were brawls over broken chairs.
A poltergeist with a playful grin,
Picks up the broom, lets mischief in.

So tap the wall, give it a cheer,
For every jest remains quite clear.
These hidden truths behind the wood,
Are all the giggles we once stood.

Memories Carved into the Foundation

In the cellar where secrets brew,
Footprints of laughter in times anew.
Cracks hold tales of cheese and wine,
And all those kids who were late for dinner time.

A potato sack race gone awry,
Laughter erupted, oh my, oh my!
Banana peels lay flat as can be,
As the foundation chuckles in glee.

Old stains of jam on the floor,
Remember the day the dog hit the door.
Hash browns danced in joy and fright,
As forks flew during breakfast fights.

So place your ear where the beams sigh,
Hear the joy from ages gone by.
Memories held where the shadows play,
A wacky jumble from yesterday.

The Weight of Shadows on Stone

Shadows linger like uninvited guests,
Hovering quietly, making their quests.
They snicker as they carefully plot,
Bringing with them the chaos they sought.

The stone walls hum with stories untold,
Of a cat with a knack for stealing the gold.
They shimmy and sway in the evening light,
Conspiring till the last door is tight.

Every crack holds a ticklish whim,
A ghostly joke, a little grin.
Lean close and ask what was the joke,
As shadows dance in a misty cloak.

So giggle with the echoes that roam,
Every shadow carries a hint of home.
The weight of these shadows, a joyful jest,
In this chamber filled with laughter, we're blessed.

Songs of the Forgotten Hearth

By the hearth where flames once danced,
Old socks lay by, unplanned and chanced.
Whispers of pie that no one could bake,
And tales of the cat that made the hearth shake.

The kettle howls with a song quite bold,
Echoing jokes from the days of old.
Each flicker and pop, a note on the air,
Sings of mishaps with an oven to spare.

The logs crackle, giving cheeky winks,
As if they know what time thinks,
Their warmth remembers each clumsy feat,
Like spilled soup during a family meat.

So gather 'round, listen with glee,
For the hearth's old songs are a jubilee.
In the laughter of flames, we'll find our part,
Songs of the hearth live deep in the heart.

www.ingramcontent.com/pod-product-compliance
Lightning Source LLC
Chambersburg PA
CBHW060142230426
43661CB00003B/539